Dear Sister Irma Mae,

Christ's love will be with you and in you all days of your life and beyond.

Love,

Barbara

BEYOND TIME .....

..... GWEN FROSTIC

his Earth = =

      with its great green trees =
        its infinite life = =
          and boundless beauty = = =
   the only earth there'll ever be . . . .

These Waters = =

     of deep springs
       of rivers and lakes = =
       drops of dew = =
         and clouds above = = =
  all the water there has ever been = = =
      all = = = there will ever be . . . . . .

The air all around = = =

     that everything must breathe = = =
       over and over = = = = =
         forever and ever . . . . .

Love this earth = = = =

   love it as much as life itself = =
    earth from which all life has come =
      earth to which all life returns . . .
  Love its waters = = =
      and keep them clean = = = =
    water on which all life depends . . . . .
    Love clear air = = =
    care enough to keep it clear = = =
     clear enough to see the stars = = = =

And earth will remain = = =
       beyond time . . . .

Trees growing in a cluster
    tend to adopt the characteristics of the group =
    they bend and sway together = = = =
    finding their strength in unity . . . . . .

Standing alone ~~~~~~~~~~ ~ ~ ~~
    with room to spread its massive limbs = =
    a single tree finds freedom = = = =
    living with the forces of the winds = = =
                    = = the sun
    and the moving seasons = = ، ~
  it becomes a symbol of
          individuality ~ ~ ~~~~

The sunset in the western sky =
radiant leaves on the trees of fall
frost flowers at the edge of a pond = =

= = = the wild rose = =
= = = = wood lilies = = =
and Queen Anne's lace = = =

each = = = has a moment of glory
while beauty goes on
beyond time ‒ ‒ ～～～～

Spring peepers sing at twilight =
　　　　birds begin at dawn = = =
　　the notes of the crickets ring in the air = =
　　　　there's a whistle of wind in the trees at night = = =

= = multitudinous sounds blend together
　　　　　　　　and vibrate on the air = = = = =

　= = = the solo parts may change
～～～～～～～～～ but the music goes on
　　　　　　　　　　beyond time . . . . .

From green plants
　　　　　to insects = = =
　　　　　　　　to bird and animal = =

　　the endless succession continues = = = = =

　　　　as life gives way to life
～～～～～ - ～ that life may go on
　　　　　　　　beyond time . . . .

But ——— —— ————————————

> the beauty = =
>   the music = = =
>   and life itself = = = =

will go on beyond time
           only if man comes to
                understand the urgency

> of preserving
>   the land = =
>   = = the water = = =
>   and the very air . . . .

Only if he finds a way
      of correlating his needs
           with those of the universe

> will there be
>   any time
>   beyond now - - ~~~~~~

The weed shall survive - - -
attuned to the winds -
the sun and
many soils . . . .
Through storms
droughts
and all adversities -
these wild WILD plants
will prevail . . . !

its beginning each life
is beautiful and promising . . . .

A new leaf reaching for the light = =
the little duck swimming on the pond = =
each baby animal in the woods = = = =

born with energy and vitality
a zest for life . . . . . .

As the dynamics of its natural growth expand =
it becomes an inseparable part of its milieu = = = =
utilizing the resources accessible

to become = = =

and to flourish . . . .

It will venture = =

always reaching beyond = =

and it must conserve = =

it must not destroy the things
that gave it life

or it will destroy itself ⁓

Each individual must develop a
flexibility to adapt to adversity = = =
and a wondrous resilience
and capacity to heal itself . . . .

There will be great competition
from those of its own = =
= it will fight for life =
and room for its survival . . . . .

It will not
by choice = =
give its life for another = = =
that is not a choice
any living thing can make ⌒

$\mathcal{L}$ife is precarious =
            it demands vigor and fitness
        and always
                coming to terms with limitations . . . . .

It demands living without rejection = =
        that all time and energy be spent on growth . . .

        It begins with beauty = =
                        = = and promise =
            it must fulfill that promise
                or perish along the way ⁓ ⁓ ⌁

Feel the excitement and grandeur of a storm = = =
                    = = the ominous rushing of the winds
                            = snow drifting = = =
                                    snowflake upon snowflake
                    each = a unique and perfect crystal
                                        made of water . . . . .

Sense the calm and beauty of a starlit night = = =
            as the milky way spans the sky
                with a myriad individual stars = = =
                    shining in the great vastness of space . . . .

        See a little frog = =
                            wait in statuesque stillness for a fly = = =
                    tiptoe by = = =
                                not to disturb his waiting = = = = =

= or = watch him make his catch = = =
and feel not pity for the loser =
but sense the triumph of the winner = =
with assurance that all is well
in life's vast complicated way
in which each life must sometime meet an end
= that life shall always beautify
the earth . . .

L isten to the bird calls of springtime
= = and feel a simple communion
without words . . .

S ee flowers blossoming in the summer fields
and understand the passion
each one has to grow . . . .

Watch a deer at twilight = = =
a tiny mouse with bright and sparkling eyes =
= a spider spin its web of silk = = = =
aware that the same life that flows
through each of them
flows through all men – – ～～～～
that each thing has its rightful niche to fill = = =
= = = each is fulfilling a vital need . . . . .

And in a moment of solitude = = =
beside a quiet pond =
feel the merging of your soul
with its serenity . . . . . .

Fly with a gull across the lake
                   as sunlight colors the western sky = =
           catch a glimpse of the grandeur of creation = = =
       = = = envision the spirit of life
                   exemplified in every living thing . . . . . .

Keep the wondrous spirit of wonder = = =
                           = = = = = always . . .

For the call of the winds = =
               the love in the songs
                       of the birds and the insects = = =
                   the joyousness of the woods
                           and the open fields = = = =
               reach those attuned to the timeless
                           rhythm of the universe = = =
           those who understand
                   and love it all
                           as one . . . .

A little violet in the woods of spring is derived
from many violets that met the challenge of life
and brought this blossom into being . . . .

*T*his is the secret of the rhythm of the flowers = =
the continual miracle by which all life evolves
and strives for excellency . . . .

*T*here is a destiny that will not deprive life's best
that the weak may survive = = = = but endows
all with astounding potentialities = = = = and
lets each live unto itself . . . .

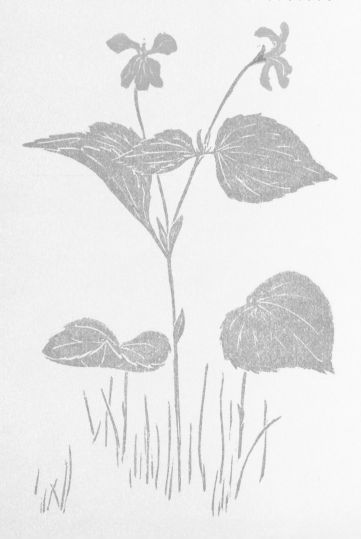

*S*pring becomes summer = = = =
and a myriad seeds are released . . . .

Seeds so packed with life . . . . .

One may become a great tree = = = another =
become food for other life = = = each = vital to
the endless procession of the universe . . . . . .

*F*rom the time life = so carefully packed within
the little seed = begins = = = it must grow = =
its leaves must seek the light = = = its roots
reach out for food = = together they achieve a
delicate balance of restoration and adjustment
= = = = = as long as the plant shall live
it must grow = =

= = = for what is life
but growth ⸺ ?

With a simple lichen on a rock
or the most complex organism that lives = = =

⸺ to stay growth
is to kill life ⸺ ⸺ ⸺ ⸺

*F*rom the beginning of life on earth = = =
growth and the quest for perfection
has been the one consistency . . . .

A falling leaf
witch hazel
mushrooms
— autumn
— the awareness
of the timelessness of nature . . .

*W*e stand now = = =
↑ where no man has stood before = =
= = at the brink of destruction
by our own hands ————

We must come to understand
the delicate balance by which
life has survived for
unknown years . . . . . .

Know the relationship of the
owl to the mouse = = =
= = the bees to the clover = = = =
and all things =
to the green plants upon this earth . . . .
Know that when a tree is cut
= a crucial link in purifying the air
has been destroyed . . . . .

Let each thing fill its vital niche = = =
each bird = =
caterpillar or snail = = =
the floods of spring
and storms = =
knowing that
only in our limited vision
are they destructive . . . .

Realize that man
is part of that balance = = =
that things do not exist
for man alone . . . .

We must create a great change
in human direction = = =

= an understanding
of the interdependency
by which the universe evolves . . . . .

Know
= = that knowing = = = = = =
is the underlying foundation
for the life we must develope . . . . .

We cannot leave it to the scientists = =
nor any form of government = = = =

each individual
must fuse a philosophy
with a plan of action

that will harmonize
with the elements . . . . . .

o one
   n o w = = =
         can justify destruction
               in the name of progress . . . .

For progress can only come
      as we correlate with
      th e forces of the universe
            for the common good of all . . . . . .

We must not turn backward
            to find our way = = =

         but by persistence = =
            = = and insistence = = =
               engineer creative procedures
                  that will not include destruction . . . .

Let no one deny the problem
            = = = = nor dare to say
                        it is not *his* = = = =
         he is the plague of all *mankind* . . . .

We must bring about
a total interplay of all our senses = = =

= = develope a deep reverence for life = = =
that will not let us
crush a growing plant = =
nor kill a little spider
= = = simply because it's there = =

but lets us understand
that the web that it is spinning
is a necessary strand
in the great web in which
all life is involved . . . . .

As individuals
we must seek a new consciousness

= = = = we are not spectators = = =
the fight is ours

= = = = = now . . . . . .

In the individual
           as in the universe
                    order is a profound necessity . . . .

Snow covers the fields = = =
              = each twig and weed
                       twinkles in the morning light = = =
           and = as the last winds of winter
                              fade into an echo = = =
              the rustle of spring begins . . . .
Summer blends into fall
              and the humming finale of the insects
                       rises from the tangled grasses . . . . . .

Methodically
           season follows season = = =
           night follows day = = = =
                 and the moon and stars move
                       in their unwavering pattern . . . . .

Fringed gentians open to the morning light
                 and close as the sun reaches its height = =
           = there are other plants
                 that blossom only in the darkness
                                of night = =
              their eternal rhythm perpetuated
                       by the nocturnal moths . . . .

Redwings leave and return each year
in a cycle of regularity
guided by a sensitivity
to all the forces of their surroundings . . . .

The tempo of all life
is attuned to order = = =
a sequential system
all things must observe . . . . . .

Plants = animals = =
and all the things of earth = = =
live with an inborn sense of regularity = =
= keyed to the harmonious order
of the universe . . . . . .

The acceptance of regularity
= = = without revulsion = = = =
is the fountainhead
of freedom . . . .

There is always a gradual = =
   almost imperceptible transformation in the air . . . .

Insects =
   having passed through their many phases = =
   will complete the final cycle of their lives =
   = leaving eggs that will assure the unbroken
                  succession of their kind . . . .

Trees draw water back into their roots
         in preparation for their period of rest . . .
Other green plants release their seeds
   and become dry stalks waving
              in the winds . . . .

It's a sensitivity to all the little stimuli
              in their environment
   that sends the birds on their long
         flights across land and seas . . . . . .

The whole earth was formed = = = =
   = = = and is developing = =
   by slow = = = = very slow
              succession . . . . . .

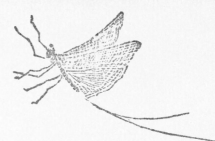

The ice age came and receded so gradually that life
        living at that time could not have known
                    that anything was happening . . .

It created great lakes and rolling hills = = =
        lakes and hills that are continuing their
            transformation even unto this day . . . .

A continuous drifting of climate
                affects all the living earth . . . .

A shifting of the rains and the winds = = = =
    = = and seeds and spores of countless
                plants are borne in new directions . . . . .

        Rocks become sand = = = =
                    lakes become meadows . . . . .

Change shapes the future = = =
                        as it created today . . . .

    Not through sudden spectacular moves
                = = = = never by chance = = =
        but always = = =
                through the inevitable process
                            of evolution . . . . .

The life that shall flourish
            will be the life
                that adapts to its environment
                    = = = and its changes . . . . . .

    Not one that tries to make
                the world conform to its needs
        = = = and sets out to redesign the universe
                    in one grand gesture . . . . . .

    The life that shall thrive
            will be the outgrowth of what has been = = =
                growing = each hour = to what shall be . . .

    A life =
            with true sensitivity to its surroundings = =
                that lives and grows within the realm
                    of simple change . . .

wild storm rages — ---
- winds reach violent proportions
thunder crashes to the earth..

Great trees bend and sway - -
leaves fly -
branches break - -
but the roots will hold —

And when the storm
has spent its fury - - -
when the winds have subsided
there will be a time of freshness
- a time of new growth . . .

The trees will stand erect -
the sun will shine again
- and
- from the topmost branch
a warbler will sing —

A hummingbird = = =

= = a crow = = =

both birds = =

with feet and bills

= = with feathers and wings = = =

yet different = = = = = =

seeking different foods

flying different airways

each living unto itself = = =

with no desire to dominate or control the other . . .

Neither is better

= = = = nor more important

= = = just = different . . . .

That variation that lets all life

live harmoniously

upon this earth . . . . . .

A huge chestnut = = =

= = a delicate poplar = = = =

each a tree = =

with roots in the earth = = =

= = trunks and limbs reaching . . . .

The chestnut developes its great massive limbs slowly
= = = spreading far over the land
for many years . . . . . .

The poplar grows rapidly
in spots where other trees could not survive = = =
its leaves shimmer
with the slightest breeze . . . . .

Each = = left to its own resources =
will assure the continuance of its kind . . . . .

Each equal = = =
in beauty = =
in its unique place in the universe =
= = equal = = = and different . . . .

And so it is = = =
with all the things of earth = =
each developing its own pattern of life = = =
= = = each is sustained by
and sustains other life = = =
as the wondrous cycle
of material and energy transformation
supports the living universe . . . .